Common Sense

And Other Bits
of Wisdom we
Tend to Forget
or Ignore

LOUISE SMITH

ISBN-13: 978-0-9842847-8-8

ISBN-10: 0-9842847-8-8

Cover and interior designed by Joel Friedlander
www.TheBookDesigner.com

Milverstead Publishing LLC
31 Rampart Drive
Wayne, PA 19087
(888)667-3981

Visit us on the web!
www.milversteadpublishing.com

For all of you.
Thank you for the inspiration!

⚜

Introduction
To me...and to Common Sense

I couldn't even begin to count the number of wise-cracks I made about my part-time, no-brainer, semi-retirement gig as a lift operator at the local ski resort's tubing park.

My gosh, I was a corporate girl. I'd seen much success in my life. Even published a book. So, when the subject of my new employment would come up, I was the first to offer a quip.

They said it would be a physical job. Pfft! I ran marathons for crying out loud. Twenty six point two miles! I mountain biked six days a week – and

I even had a half ironman under my belt. Physical job? I cracked a joke.

They said I had to be gracious to the guests. Whaaat?!?!? I invented customer service and couldn't imagine any possible conditions that would render me unkind. I cracked a joke.

They mentioned I'd have to like the outdoors as the shifts were seven solid hours of being in the wintery elements. I coughed at the absurdity of me not wanting to be outdoors all day long. I lived in the bush! I am an outdoor fanatic. I cracked another joke.

I even cracked a joke when I realized my entire new 'team' consisted of a brood of teenaged boys.

For those who haven't experienced winter tubing, picture a large hill, extremely steep incline covered with snow, and sculpted into six individual lanes.

People pay money to sit in a big rubber tube and be pushed down the icy lanes.

It is exhilarating. I know. I am now a Tube Thrower. I am the person perched at the top, doing the pushing, spinning, pulling. The person responsible for the ultimate ride of a lifetime.

My first shift started off with an abundance of confidence. Throwing on two lanes at a time, I vaulted over the ice wall separating the two lanes with the prowess of an Olympic hurdles gold medal winner.

I pushed. I pulled. I spun. I leapt over the wall and repeated the process.

Layers of clothing were cast aside as I heated up and sweat poured off me. Each time a rider asked for a straight, fast run, I pushed so hard I ended up half way down the hill.

Trying to stop after letting the tube go is like sliding to a stop on a skating rink. Digging in the knees, feet and hands, I could only pray that some part of my appendages would grip onto something so I wouldn't have to hike back up the entire hill.

Climbing back up the hill. It was sort of like conquering Everest. A thousand times in one day.

In the beginning my head would pop back up in view of the waiting tubers like a gopher popping out of a hole. Cheers would go up! Arms would pump in victory.

Somewhere along the way I realized that a pile of men, all wanting to hang onto each other's tube for the ride of their life, was like hauling a thousand pounds of dead weight. Spinning them, and getting out of the way in time, turned out to require more finesse and delicate grace than a ballet dancer and speed skater combined.

After a few hours, my finesse drained and the Everest climbs all ran into one barely recognizable strain.

Vaulting the ice wall became more of a desperate slither, although I did notice, with clarity at one point, that ice really is as hard as a rock!

I recall one time clawing my way back up the hill, uncertain if I was still living or if I had in fact died and God decided I needed to work a little harder before letting me pass through the pearly gates.

I clawed up not certain my fingers were still attached. I prayed with all my might for a forty pound six year old to be waiting for me.

I got to the top. Begged my legs to follow me over the ice wall. I raised my weary eyes, and there, all set up, ready and raring was a group of six men, six tubes, and a good hour of beer-drinking under their belt. They were twenty feet from the edge of the hill.

This was six hours into my seven hour shift. I think I let out a cry as I shook my head and hollered, momentarily forgetting the rules of pleasant customer service, 'Are you FREAKING NUTS?!?!? I ain't pushin' ya from back there! She-ite!! – you must weight a TON!!! Get up and bring your tubes closer to me!'

One of my fellow Throwers laughed so hard he fell over.

Lucky for me, the men did too. I praised the mind-deadening attributes of beer. That group of guys wanted the ride of their life, and they got it. I know this because they came back again and again and again.

Eventually I heard the magical words that my shift was over.

I hugged my loyal tubers (who knew they developed alliances and favourites), and I staggered over to where the spare tubes were kept. It was one last ride down for me before I could fall into the bliss of my bed.

"Yo, Weez! You lucky dude (apparently I am a forty-something year old female dude), you get to turtle down - there are no spare tubes," hollered one of the brood.

Before I knew what was happening, I was lying on my back, legs pulled into my chest and throttling myself down the hill, head first.

No one is allowed to do that. I can see why.

When my body finally came screeching to a stop, I stood, albeit wobbly, attempted to focus my eyes and trudged to my car. It was covered with snow. I barely noticed. I was delirious. I think.

I opened the door. Turned my butt to the seat and fell in. My legs didn't follow.

I mustered a bit of reserve energy, grabbed each leg above the knee one at a time, and lifted them in, scowling as I remembered I drove stick-shift. Damn clutch.

Eventually I made it home. Eventually I got out of the car. Eventually I went to bed, and this is where common sense of the day comes into play.

Someday, sometime, when you least expect it, fate will get you back for your wise-crack jokes, so be careful what you make fun of. It'll always come back and haunt you!

Three thoughts went through my tired brain as I laid flat on my back in bed that night, unable to move a single muscle.

First, I thought about how much I actually liked the job.

Second, I thought about the payback for all my wise-cracks and the hilarity of it all. I got exactly what I deserved!

My third thought was a little selfish. I sort of wished I had installed a crane in the bedroom that could roll me over onto my side.

Life is a journey my friends. We are all born with the same common sense. Whether we remember it, heed it, or learn from it is what distinguishes us from each other.

It is my hope this book will help you remember any long-lost or ignored common sense. We've all been there at some point in time!

Enjoy,
Louise

*I*F I HAVE LEARNED ANYTHING in this life it is this: the world is beautiful, peace revolves around kindness, and although I am only one voice, I am a voice!

☙

KNOWLEDGE AND WISDOM IS NOT the same thing. Knowledge comes from the lessons we learn in life, school, books, and work. Wisdom comes from how you use that knowledge. Wisdom is your decision to act a certain way, or not act at all, after considering the welfare of everyone involved.

☙

*W*HEN YOU END A RELATIONSHIP, you end an *us* cycle. It is imperative you spend time in a new *me* cycle as you will be different. You need to learn who the new *me* is, what *you* like, what *your* goals are, who *you* want to be. You need to be *happy* as a *me*. You cannot jump into the arms of another us until you are – or things will unravel again.

⚜

*N*EVER RELY ON OTHERS FOR happiness, self-worth or contentment. If you can't *love* and *respect* yourself, others will find you less lovable too. First step – *accept* yourself for you who are *right now.* The good and bad. Change anything *you* see fit, because *you* want it, not because someone else wants it. Being happy with self is the key to being happy with all else.

⚜

$\mathcal{I}$F YOU STOP BELIEVING IN miracles, how will they ever come true? No matter what is going on in your life, no matter how happy you may be in some areas, and unhappy in others, *always* keep a clear image of what you desire in your mind and heart. Doing so costs nothing and may just pay off in the long run!

⚜

COMMON SENSE • *Louise Smith*

*F*OCUS ON WHAT IS MEANINGFUL in your life - think of things that *always* bring you peace, calm and joy. Expand on those. Let go of the things that are not meaningful or cause you pain, anger, sadness or to argue. Spending too much time and/or head-space on them is stopping you from having more of the meaningful!

⚕

*T*HERE WILL BE DAYS WHEN outer noise pushes and pulls at your very core. On those days it is important to know the drama is just that. Drama. Stay clear. Calm your breathing. Center yourself and ride out the storm knowing not every wave needs to crash into your shore.

⚓

*I*F YOU FOLLOW YOUR GUT (vibes, intuition, inner 'knowing') you will never let others manipulate you into doing what you know is not fair, just or right for you. Manipulation comes in many styles including big smiles and kind, yet pleading words. It is ***imperative*** you stop, listen and heed your gut feelings or you may end up taking a wrong turn.

⚓

$\mathscr{W}$HEN FACED WITH AGGRESSIVE ANGRY words/actions from another, respond from a calm and peaceful place, and not in a reactive, defensive manner. Be calm. Breathe deeply.

A hard lesson to learn in this life is to be kind even when others seem undeserving.

When you learn to be the peacekeeper of your own mind, body, and soul (your words/actions/thoughts), less and less negativity comes near you.

⚜

O F ALL THINGS YOU REQUIRE courage for in this journey of life, you require the most courage to be *yourself!* In a world that constantly makes demands on you, your thoughts, beliefs, commitments, dreams and interests, it takes incredible power, concentration and belief that you are worth it to *stay true to yourself.* If you don't, no one will. Best of luck my friends!

☙

IF YOU WANT HONESTY IN your life – be honest.

If you want joy – be joyful.

If you want contentment – be content.

If you want happy, joyful, wonderful people in your life – offer them the same.

⚜

$\mathcal{T}$RUE GIVING, AT THE MOST profound and fulfilling level comes when we do it with absolutely no expectation for anything in return.

Giving from the heart, whether it is your time, your services, talents or purchased items becomes truly a gift of love, respect and honour, when you have absolutely no expectation to receive anything for it. Not a return gift. Not a card. Not a thank you. Not even an acknowledgement.

When you leave all expectations at the door. When you step away from 'wanting something' and let the receiver do with it what they will, then, you will have mastered the lesson of giving.

⚜

$\mathcal{W}$E ALL END RELATIONSHIPS IN this journey through life, whether it's friends, lovers, or spouses. If you do, remember this - you *cannot* successfully jump into the arms of another 'us' until you are 100% happy and content with *you!* If you do jump, the issues that plagued you before *will* rear their ugly head again. Discover who the *new you* is - be proud - be happy - *then* a new 'us' is possible.

$\mathscr{B}$EFORE YOU CAST A JUDGING eye at another for their words, actions or behaviour, do a quick check of your own to make sure your saintly halo is still untarnished! Remember - what we find 'wrong' with others, always ends up being a shadow of ourselves.

☩

$\mathcal{W}$HEN THINGS DON'T SEEM TO be lining up or moving forward 'out there,' it's a good time to quiet your head and heart and focus on 'inner growth and expansion.'

Look inside - are you kind? Mean? Content? Bitter?

Do you blame others for your lot in life?

Recognize that everything you have experienced makes you either *better* or *bitter.*

Let go of the bitter - and acknowledge *how* the experience made you *better!*

⚜

"THERE IS NOTHING LIKE RETURNING TO A PLACE THAT REMAINS UNCHANGED TO FIND THE WAYS IN WHICH YOU YOURSELF HAVE ALTERED."

~ *Nelson Mandela.*

Truer words were never spoken! As we travel through this journey of life, we will be filled with opportunity to grow. It really does boil down to a choice between being better or bitter. Choose wisely.

*W*HEN FACED WITH LISTENING TO either your head or your heart, choose neither. Instead slow yourself down, breathe deeply, calm your mind, and then listen and rely on your intuition. Your gut feelings. Your inner 'knowing.' Your vibes. This is how you will stay on the right path!

⚜

*I*F YOU RELY ON SOMETHING or someone to supply a place of happiness, you haven't found it yet. Happiness occurs when your heart and head are at peace, no matter what is going on, where you are, what you are doing and who you are with.

❧

$\mathscr{I}$F YOU GOSSIP ABOUT PEOPLE, people will gossip about you! Why does that always seem so surprising to those that speak ill, fabricate or spread hearsay? If you want to live a life of peace, contentment and calm, you *must* let go of the need to be attached to other people's business. If you crave drama, pick up a good book instead!

⚜

MOMENT CHANGES EVERYTHING. WHEN THIS occurs my friends, make certain you are calm not defensive, observing, not absorbing. The world will often change your direction for you -... so flow *with* it, knowing everything is happening as it is supposed to.

As YOU FORGE A PATH in the direction of a *new you* - spend time with those who support and share your ideas. Stay away from those who dismiss your feelings, ideas and dreams and pull you into their world. It's okay to have different dreams than others. Stay true to what feels right for you - sharing them with those who will kindly support you!

⚜

*I*MAGINE YOU GOT A CAR when you were born, but were told it was the only one you would get your *entire life!*

Would you pour junk in the tank and expect it to run well?

The same applies to your body. If you fill your belly/ tank with junk, your engine *will* sputter, putt and conk out at the side of the road.

This is the *only* body you will get – rest it, fuel it with care - treat it like the prized possession it is!

⚜

*D*o you want to be *more* positive? Start using the words, 'wouldn't it be nice.'

Instead of 'I hate this job' ~switch to~ 'Wouldn't it be nice if I liked this job.'

Or 'The kids are driving me *crazy!*' ~to~ 'Wouldn't it be nice if the kids didn't drive me crazy.'

By putting those four words in front of your sentences/thoughts, you train your mind to be *positive*.

This *will* change your life.

Simple isn't it!

⚜

*I*T'S OKAY TO SAY 'NO thank you' to invitations, particularly from friends and family who create stressful environments for you. Forcing yourself to spend time with them will only interfere with your serenity. Don't let feelings of guilt or obligation interfere with your sanity! You are *worth* it!

⚜

$\mathcal{W}$HAT IS STOPPING YOU FROM living happily? What fear or insecurity are you allowing to anchor you in the past? Are you confident in knowing that you *deserve* a life of contentment?

The key to living in a happy state is noticing that wonderful things occur all around you each and every day. Spend your time acknowledging and enjoying these gifts and your 'happy list' will soon outgrow your 'misery list.'

SOMETIMES WE CREATE OUR OWN nightmares. Sometimes we refuse to listen to our gut, and we ignore the 'no' grumbling deep within or the 'yes' that's calling to our hearts.

We often do this because we feel guilt, or we put other's feelings or needs ahead of our own.

Sometimes we believe we are not worth it, and don't deserve anything better.

⚓

*W*HEN YOU STAY ON A path that is past it's proverbial 'due date', or you allow yourself to feel undeserving, or that someone else's needs are more important than your own, the winds of life start to blow and the storms intensify.

Listen to your intuition - it will always lead you in the *right* direction!

You are worth it.

You deserve nothing less than a magical, fulfilling and peaceful life of joy!

⚜

YOU WON'T ALWAYS BE RIGHT, yet it is so hard for some to admit when they've made a mistake or hurt another. Apologizing is NOT a sign of weakness. It's exactly the opposite - a sign of incredible strength and honour as you take ownership of your actions, and a willingness to live with the consequences. In apology you learn a lesson in being humble.

Wishing someone else would apologize?

Maybe it's not your call on whether someone else apologizes or not. We each have our own journey - and far be it for anyone to decide what is or isn't right for someone else's. Although it might make sense to you that a person apologizes, maybe there is more for them to learn before that's possible. Nothing is worse than an empty apology - where a person

41

says something out of duty, rather than of caring and taking ownership.

So, let it go.

You can't change what another person says, does, or thinks. You can only change your reaction to it.

☙

_L_ET GO OF TRADITIONS IF they are causing you stress. Like baking great grandma's shortbreads, or hosting the Christmas Cheer Drop In. If trying to fit it all in is turning your mood from joy to bitterness, and resentment - *then change things up!* If we never changed our 'traditions' we'd still be gathered around fires, waiting for the hunters to return to the cave.

⚜

*K*INDNESS IS CONTAGIOUS. YOU NEVER know when your smile or kind word will land *exactly* where it's needed! If you feel inclined to be moody, miserable and negative, we only ask you to keep your distance from the rest of us. That would be the kind thing to do!

⚜

*I*N THE HEIGHT OF A life storm, sometimes the best you can do is hunker down, stay calm and wait till the worst is over. After the winds die down, look around, see the different paths in front of you, and follow one. Maybe you'll rebuild. Maybe you'll walk on. Either way, in *that* moment, you need to acknowledge what you learned, be grateful the lesson is over, and walk forward with confidence.

⚜

*F*EELING REGRET MEANS YOU DIDN'T learn the lesson. You must look for the deeper meaning (Hint: it's always something that makes *you* a better person). Once you acknowledge the lesson was learned, you feel *gratitude*, and move forward with no regrets. To ignore the lesson and keep regret attached to your mind and heart, you hold yourself in the position of having that lesson presented again another day.

⚓

Most people fill time with work-related or 'have to' activities. This causes burn-out, frustration and a loss of purpose. Schedule time every day for *you* - even if it's only five minutes - and do something *you* want to do, see or dream about. By putting yourself first you will end up having more energy for everyone else.

⚜

COMPROMISE ON THE DINNER MENU, schools, purchases, spending, time spent with the in-laws. Never compromise on integrity, honesty, dreams of the future, and kindness toward others. It's amazing how many like-minded souls you'll find along the way.

☙

YOU ARE ACCOUNTABLE FOR EVERYTHING you say and do, so say and do things you are proud of. Say and do things to make a difference in the life of other people, the natural world and the planet as a whole. Be honest, *always*. Have integrity, always. Be kind, always. *This* is the road to contentment.

✧

$\mathcal{T}$ODAY FOCUS ON HEALING CONFLICT. Name someone you have conflict with and write yourself a note describing the details of that struggle - *without* assigning blame. Focus instead on *you* (your fears, feelings, insecurities). This will help you realize remaining in conflict is a *choice* and blame, anger and resentment are dark clouds that *keep* you there. *Free yourself - move on!*

⚜

TODAY ACKNOWLEDGE YOUR OWN WISDOM. Ponder one or two of the greatest truths you've learned in your life, and use it to raise yourself and others higher. Doing so will help you discover how powerful it is when you take a life lesson from thought and put it into form or action. Enjoy the journey my friends.

☨

To WORRY IS TO BE stuck in fear. Fear of the unknown, fear of not being in control, fear things won't work out the way you want. Replace all worry with *trust*. Trust that everything happens for a reason, and trust that you ultimately aren't the one in control of the situation anyway. Putting your energy into *trust* allows peace and calm to flow through your heart and mind.

⚜

COMMON SENSE • *Louise Smith*

"WHILE I AM HERE, CONTAINED WITHIN BONES AND MUSCLES, ORGANS AND SKIN, I WANT TO TAKE CARE OF THE GIFT OF MY BODY. I WANT TO FEED IT WELL, MOVE IT GRACEFULLY, AND REST IT DEEPLY."

~ *Elizabeth Lesser.*

This is something for all of us to remember, not only during hectic holidays where many feel frazzled and out of sync, but throughout the year.

⚜

$\mathcal{B}$E CAREFUL OF FOLLOWING SOMEONE else's dreams as they sometimes leave no room for your own independent thoughts and beliefs.

I call this 'being lost in the Sea of Him or Her.'

Know what *you* want! Support others in their quests - as long as you get to stay true to yourself and your dreams while doing so.

⚜

"LIFE'S JOURNEY IS NOT TO ARRIVE AT THE GRAVE SAFELY IN A WELL PRESERVED BODY, BUT RATHER TO SKID IN SIDEWAYS, TOTALLY USED UP AND WORN OUT, SHOUTING '...MAN, WHAT A RIDE!'"

~ *George Carlin*

☙

*T*OO MUCH TIME IS WASTED thinking individually about the 'stuff' we want – clothes, cars, homes, jobs, relationships. When you change your thinking from 'what do I want ' to 'what can I do for others' - everything shifts, you discover your purpose, you exude happiness and miracles occur.

⚜

THE PATH TO CONTENTMENT BEGINS with learning to love your own company, in the good moments as well as in the bad moments.

◈

*I*T'S TIME TO STOP SEEING certain people, and your relationship with them, through rose-coloured glasses.

Stop wishing, hoping, praying, and trying to change them to be who *you* want them to be.

That's not your call!

Once you stop the 'be-who-I-want/need-you-to-be' game, you open yourself up to connecting with people who truly share your values, morals, interests, thoughts, likes, dreams, desires, and beliefs.

And you free them to find theirs, which is something they equally deserve.

It's okay to wind down a friendship or relationship if more things don't work, then do.

Have confidence in this process!

As HUMANS WE ARE CAPABLE of the greatest good and the greatest evil. Free will is what determines the path we choose. To ensure you are on the road to peace, love, joy and contentment, step away from judgment, bitterness, jealousy and anger, and practice the daily art of forgiveness, compassion, and empathy. Be the kind, loving soul you were born to be.

⚜

*H*APPINESS IS NOT A PLACE or destination. You cannot buy it, own it, earn it, wear it or give it away. You do not hunt for it, or 'find' it. Happiness IS the spiritual experience of living every minute of everyday with love, grace and gratitude.

☧

$\mathcal{T}$ODAY DO LESS. LOOK AT how much you do for others and whether you overextend yourself to the point of being unnecessarily exhausted (which can lead you to resentment). Why do you have to do it all? Deep down there is a reason you are willing to sabotage your own health - and in order to be healed, it needs to be identified.

༜

*L*AUGHTER CLEANSES THE SOUL AND lightens the load. Today assess whether you truly have a sense of humour or not. A healthy sense of humour lifts burdens, adds light where there is darkness, and allows stress to flow *away* from the body. Laugh *with* people, never *at* them. Laugh at least a dozen times *every* day - especially in difficult times!

⚜

$\mathscr{E}$ACH DAY YOU ARE A *new person!* You will have a thought, intention or awareness that helps you evolve a little every day. You need to see yourself and all your friends and family as you/they are to-day, not as they were before. Magical growth occurs when we're not looking.

$\clubsuit$

HAPPINESS IS A STATE OF INNER BEING. You won't miraculously become happy if someone else changes or if things in your world or the greater world change. You will be happy when *you* change. Change the way you see things, the way you think. Change your beliefs or your actions. Be grateful the road to *happiness* rests in *your* hands!

☙

*T*ODAY IDENTIFY A DREAM YOU have postponed. Ask yourself why? A *reason* leaves you happy/at peace as the dream is still on the agenda. An *excuse* leaves you bitter/resentful toward *whatever* you think is holding you back. An *excuse* is negativity (blaming). *Believe* it's viable. Believe you are worth it. If you don't know how and when it will come to be, simply *enjoy* dreaming/imagining *that it will!*

⚜

*T*ODAY IS THE DAY TO start empowering yourself. Choose the attitude you will allow to flow through you - positive or negative. This means you *choose* your mood! Choose the way you react to others. Choose what words/thoughts ebb from your lips/ mind. Choose who/what helps you live in positivity (and kindly remove the rest). Today is the day you realize *you* have the power and ability to flow in goodness!

⚜

My DEAR FRIEND SONYA HAD terminal cancer. It's a tough go when the doctors tell you your time left on earth is limited. Yet, I watched and listened with amazement as she lived each day with gusto, enthusiasm and an intense desire to see and do all she could in whatever time she had left.

The ticking clock was ticking, the pain was unrelenting, the strain overwhelming at times, yet she was happy and thankful for all that life was giving her.

We should all live like that.

~ *In loving memory of Sonya Mensink* ~

☙

SPRING IS NATURE'S WAY OF reminding us seasons change; dark, cold nights end, and new growth comes. The same applies to life. We must let go of things that happened last year, last month, or yesterday, if we want fresh new growth to appear in our lives. Follow nature's lead, learn from it – let it go – and watch new life spring forth!

⚓

$\mathscr{P}$EOPLE LOOK AT SPRING WITH hopes for a new start. If you want different results, you need to change last year's behaviour. It doesn't get any simpler than that.

♱

*I*F YOU'RE IN A RUT - change things up.

Change your routines; what you eat for breakfast, lunch, dinner.

Change what you do after work, or before.

Change who you sit with, what you talk about, or who you hang out with at night.

Change the programs you watch, the activities you do.

You can even change your mind!

You'll never know what amazing things are waiting unless you switch it up!

⚓

*D*O NOT REGRET YESTERDAY.

It's done.

Over.

Past.

Acknowledge the lessons, and move on.

Do not fear tomorrow, it hasn't arrived yet.

Trust it will come as it is supposed to.

Live every moment of right now with kindness, love, honesty and integrity without picking and choosing what, when and where you will share that energy.

Share it with all!

That is a successful human life.

⚜

*Y*OU CAN GREATLY REDUCE YOUR daily problems by letting go of the need to fix, help, or be involved with everyone else's. They are not yours to solve. Unless you hear the magical words 'I need your help,' assume your input is *not* required. Doing this will free up *plenty* of time to acknowledge the beautiful world around you - and *this* is a key to contentment.

♣

*L*ISTENING IS MORE THAT JUST hearing the spoken word. To truly hear another, listen with your eyes, nose, ears, heart and spirit. You'll be amazed at how much you learn in a room full of silence.

⚜

The best way to help someone take responsibility for their own life is to stop solving their problems for them. Doing so may feel like you are letting them 'fail,' but by getting out of the equation all together, you are actually helping them learn some of the biggest lessons of life. By 'solving' everything for them, you are helping to delay the lessons.

⚜

SOCIETY TEACHES US TO JUDGE.

People by appearance, possessions by value, the day by the weather, health by pain.

Judgement is to decide right from wrong.

To be in a place of peace and contentment, we need to put all judgements aside and master the art of 'observing.'

This allows us the freedom to stay out of the equation and see the world around us as being equal and with purpose, even if we don't understand what that purpose is.

⚜

YOU DON'T NEED ANYONE'S APPROVAL in the way you live your life. Likewise, you don't need to approve or disapprove of anyone else's choices either. We are all free to be confident in who we are, what we like and where our intuition leads us. We just need courage to follow it.

⚓

"DEPRESSION IS NOURISHED BY A LIFETIME OF UN-GRIEVED AND UNFORGIVEN HURTS"

~ *Penelope Sweet.*

When hurt we surround ourselves with protective walls to 'stop it from happening again.' These walls cause you to miss learning valuable lessons from whatever caused the pain. Let the walls down, grieve whatever was lost and forgive whatever created the hurt. You will reach contentment by doing so.

☙

$\mathcal{T}$HE MOST IMPORTANT LOVE IS love of self. If you cannot love yourself unconditionally, you cannot open your heart enough to love any other. Do not wait until a more perfect you arrives. In terms of soul lessons, you are exactly where you are supposed to be, a student in the classroom of life. Stop waiting for your lessons to be finished and you to be 'perfect' - you are a perfect student right now!

In life there will be many situations for you to learn the lessons of tolerance, patience, acceptance, kindness, love, self-respect, integrity, confidence, honesty, etc. If you don't learn the lesson, it will present itself again. And again. And again. You will know you passed the test when you feel immense gratitude for the situation that created the lesson, no matter how difficult or painful it was.

⚜

IT TAKES MORE WORK TO be miserable than to be happy. Why? Because miserable people love company...which means your energy is drained from battling through all their woes as well as your own. Remove yourself from this cycle by training your mind to focus on all the *good* in your days, and let the miserable people drift away from your life.

⚜

"I HAVE NEVER MET A MAN SO IGNORANT THAT I COULDN'T LEARN SOMETHING FROM HIM."

~ *Galileo.*

No one died and made us God, and rather than judge another for their actions or inactions, we need to step back, ask why it bothers us so, and be open to learning the lesson that has been placed before us. This will happen daily in this earthly life we live.

⚜

GREET EVERYONE YOU ENCOUNTER WITH kindness. Doing so might not solve all your problems, but it sure will make you feel good about yourself for taking the high road! Plus - added bonus - kindness keeps negativity at bay. Your own, and from others!

⚓

BIRTH AND DEATH.

The cycle of life.

Letting go of someone who has passed is one of the most difficult journeys a person will take.

Today I woke up with a skip in my step and a grin on my face as I celebrate my brother Mark and the lessons I learned when he passed away suddenly at age 49.

He was a great brother in life and a most incredible spirit in death.

I am blessed!

☙

*W*HEN THE UNEXPECTED HAPPENS AND the direction of your life journey changes, you MUST let go of the old plans and make new ones. Holding on to the old ones will stall everything.

⚓

ONE OF THE BIGGEST FEARS of human kind (next to death and public speaking) is letting the walls come down so others can see who you *really* are, instead of what you think others want you to be.

When you let go of the fear that you're 'not good enough' and finally stand on a rooftop and shout - *this is me!* - Then you will be led to contentment.

⚜

$\mathcal{I}$T IS ABSOLUTELY NORMAL TO start something new with giddy excitement, only to discover it no longer feels 100% right a little further down the road.

This does *not* mean you have done something wrong or are 'bad.'

Life is a series of cycles with beginnings, middles and ends. Each cycle provides lessons for personal growth. As each cycle comes to an end, reflect on what you learned and move on.

⚜

$\mathcal{A}$N APOLOGY DOESN'T CHANGE HISTORY, but it does offer an opportunity for a different future if it's sincere, lessons were learned and changes made.

⚜

WHEN YOU ARE BORN YOU are given a body.

Don't waste precious time hating it for its limitations and imperfections - it's the only one you get.

Instead, treat it like precious gold.

Honour it, feed it well, rest it often, and praise it for doing everything you ask of it.

When you treat your body with love and respect, you complete a lesson and move forward in your journey to peace and contentment.

☙

LIFE IS LIKE A RIVER. Calm and peaceful at times. Turbulent and out of control at others. The trick is learning not to try to overpower or control the twists, turns and rapids, but to know when to pull up the oars, when to paddle and to *always* flow with the current - wherever it takes you.

༓

STRETCH YOURSELF. DO SOMETHING NEW, difficult and exciting. In doing so you will rid yourself of petty fears, doubts and judgements. You will become conscious of your own strengths - both physical and mental. You will feel a tremendous surge of spiritual growth as you realize you *are* capable, strong and good!

☙

COMMON SENSE • *Louise Smith*

NOTHING EVER STAYS THE SAME. Not people, animals, places or things. So stop trying to keep things the way they were. Change your mind, your heart, your goals, your *attitude!* Change directions, friends, interests. Life is one big daily *change* - so jump out of the box and enjoy becoming the *new you!*

⚓

$\mathcal{I}$ ABSOLUTELY LOVE THIS QUOTE.

"THERE ARE ONLY TWO WAYS TO LIVE YOUR LIFE.
ONE IS AS THOUGH NOTHING IS A MIRACLE. THE
OTHER IS AS IF EVERYTHING IS."

~ *Albert Einstein, physicist*

THERE ARE FIVE LANGUAGES OF love (ways we naturally convey our feelings of love).

Words.
Touch.
Quality Time.
Acts of Service.
Gifts.

You speak one better than all the others. Understanding your preference and the preference of others makes all the difference in effectively communicating your love. Relationships can break down when people have no idea what language their partner speaks.

⚜

TODAY I AM FEELING GRATITUDE.

For great friends,

Loving family.

A warm home, food, shelter.

There will be moments in your journey where you question 'why,' 'why me' or 'why them.'

Let your heart lead you into helping all of mankind with no expectations for anything in return.

That is a lesson of love.

⚜

THERE ARE CONSEQUENCES FOR EVERYTHING you say, think and do. Good and bad. What a good consequence is for you, may seem to be a bad one for someone else. And vice versa. Live life with integrity, honesty and kindness towards everyone, and the consequences will fall where they should.

⚜

YOU NEEDN'T WORRY WHAT OTHERS think. If what you are doing feels *right* to *you,* and it's *not* harming yourself, others, humanity or the environment around you, then you need not be concerned with the opinions of others. You are *free* to live your life in your own chosen happy state!

☙

*L*ET GO OF TRYING TO control others.

Their actions, words, decisions or past errors.

Why is it necessary for you to control the direction they go or outcome they meet?

What do you fear if that power is lost?

Recognize how much stress flows through your body when you fight to keep power and control of another's actions, thoughts, words.

Letting go will free you up to other more fun pursuits!

ODAY IDENTIFY ONE PIECE OF unfinished business (it could relate to a person, place, thing or experience), and then do something to bring closure to it. If you find you are unable to, at the very least you have found a major block in your healing. Remember, every experience in your life with either make your bitter or better. You choose!

☙

*I*T IS NOT WRONG TO question our choices and actions of the past. Quite contrary, it is a good thing to do. It opens us up to learning the valuable lessons that were placed before us.

Life isn't a perfect journey where only good things happen to good people because they do good things. It's a collection of highs and lows. Of good times and bad, good decisions and ones we wish we could take back. In the greater scheme of things, spending even a moment wishing those parts of our life never occurred is a colossal waste of time and keeps us from learning the forward moving lessons of life.

Instead of wishing it wasn't so, we must learn from those moments where we questioned ourselves and our decisions - so that we know how we should re-

COMMON SENSE • *Louise Smith*

act the next time the same lesson is placed before us. And it will. Until we learn it. It's the way life is.

$\mathcal{I}$F YOU WANT YOUR LIFE to change, then change it. Stop saying 'I can't because...' Change your job, your home, your city. Change your beliefs, your values, your behaviour. Change your friends, your relationships, your interests. Change your health, your activities. As much as you may think its other people, places and things holding you anchored back, the choice to change is actually in *your* hands!

⚓

TRUST THE INNER VOICE THAT resonates deep within your belly,

a voice that is trying to guide you.

Listen for the deep gurgle of a no,

or the wonderful tingling of a yes.

You need not analyze the no or yes with your logical mind,

instead simply trust a no means no and a yes means yes for forward movement on your journey.

☙

THE HARDEST WORD TO SAY or hear is *no*, but the most rewarding lessons are learned when we do. It is mandatory that you say *no* to requests that don't feel 100% right to you, regardless of the reason. This could be a lesson for you, the receiver of the '*no*' or both. It's hard, but have *faith* and *trust* it is the right thing to do!

⚜

*T*ODAY I ASK YOU TO stand strong in the face of arrogant or aggressive people. Arrogance is merely another face of fear. Stand strong, Observe without absorbing. And then walk away quickly leaving the drama behind you. Ultimately they are afraid of something, but it's not your problem to fix.

⚜

A LIFE FILLED WITH DIFFICULTY IS *not* a punishment. Sometimes the most evolved souls choose to take the most challenging paths for they are already at a higher level and therefore need a higher level of lessons.

⚜

FORGIVE YOURSELF. TO HEAL COMPLETELY (and live in peace, joy and contentment), you must forgive yourself for any injustices, hurts, wrong-doings or mistakes YOU still hold against yourself. Those moments happened long ago and are *over!* Today you must identify one area in your own life where you are angry, bitter or resentful with yourself and *love* yourself enough to *let it go.*

⚜

WHAT DO YOU WORRY ABOUT? When worrying, how much energy and strength do you lose, and what part of your body feels exhausted or stressed? Today is the day to recognize how worrying affects your health, and to counter this negative emotion with positive action and manifestations.

☙

$\mathcal{P}$AY ATTENTION TO YOUR CONVERSATIONS. Are they kind or mean-spirited? Are they full of gossip or good? Do they focus on perceived faults of others? Would they help or hinder yourself or another? Today is the day to start recognizing the type and quality of information *you* feed your mind, heart and soul.

☸

*I*F YOU LEARNED THE LESSON, but are still having trouble letting go of the person/ordeal/trauma, it's probably time to get busy doing other things. Find new or old *fun* activities, friends, or interests.

Stay *away* from *all negativity* and anything that 'triggers' a need to run back and 'hang on.'

Once the soul lesson is complete, *you* have to move your human self onward and upward!

⚓

"WHETHER YOU THINK YOU CAN OR THINK YOU CAN'T, YOU ARE RIGHT."

~ *Henry Ford*

Enjoy today. Enjoy changing directions, setting new goals, and learning from yesterday.

⚜

THERE WILL ALWAYS BE CHOICES of what you Should Do, and what you Will Do. Learning to differentiate between the two is a life lesson.

A Should Do is *not* based on other people's wants, opinions, or desires. A Should Do comes from deep within you, your gut feelings, inner instinct. Sometimes they take you in a completely different direction.

The Will Do's happen when you ignore your gut feelings; cave to the pressure of what you believe other's want of you; or do because following your gut seems like too much work.

The path of a Should Do leads to contentment, the path of a Will Do leads to greater frustration.

As you prepare for the next phase of your life, celebrate all you have done and accomplished.

Celebrate how far you have come in one year alone.

Celebrate the kindness you have shown others, the smiles when smiles were needed, the good deeds, and the help.

Now it is time for *you*.

Celebrate who you are and who you are becoming!

⚜

EVERYDAY YOU HAVE A CHOICE. Focus on the good, or focus on the bad. One will bring you peace, even in difficult times; the other will bring you difficulty even in peaceful times. The choice is yours and yours alone to make.

☙

$\mathcal{F}$IND WHAT MAKES YOU FEEL happy - and *do it!* Everyone has an activity that brings them great joy. If you haven't found it yet - keep trying new things until you uncover the perfect one. It does not matter one single teeny iota if anyone else likes it - so don't make that part of the equation. It's amazing how much our mind stops focusing on *gunk* when we're doing what we love!

⚜

We are, we have, we receive what we think. The most powerful words we form are often never said. If you want your journey to be filled with peace, joy and contentment, you must align the words that escape through your lips with those that occupy space in your head. Kindness, calm and love begin in the dreamy space of thoughts.

⚜

*T*HE WINDS OF CHANGE ARE upon us. Release your fears of change, rejection and failure or you will become bitter and resentful of the people, places and things you believed held you back. You *can do it!* Take a risk. Follow your dream. Now is the time.

⚜

$\mathcal{W}$HEN A MARRIAGE ENDS, BOTH partners must travel through all five stages of grief (denial, anger, bargaining, depression, acceptance), regardless of how the 'end' came to be. It is one of the hardest journeys of grief to travel because of the pull to stay stuck, or to revisit any one of the stages. Some stay stuck for years, decades or even their lifetime. If you want to find true peace and joy in life, you MUST complete this journey.

⚜

STAY TRUE TO YOUR BELIEFS, your dreams, your needs, and desires (even if they are changing and evolving), and the world will either flow with you or drift away. Letting go of everything and everyone that does not support you for who you are at the very core is the most cleansing, liberating and exciting thing you can do. Good luck my friends!

⚜

$\mathcal{I}$T'S NEVER A GOOD IDEA to stay resentful. Sure that person, place or thing hurt you. Maybe even on purpose. But staying bitter is giving you permission to stay anchored back in that painful place. Contemplate on what you learned from it, forgive and move on. Staying resentful and bitter doesn't hurt *them* in any way shape or form it just hurts *you* and those around you!

☙

To ACCEPT OR LAMENT.

One is the realization 'it is what it is' and there is a bigger picture.

The other keeps you feeling 'pity' in a state of 'self.'

One is a road to peace and contentment.

The other an anchor holding you in a place of pain.

⚜

WHETHER YOU LOSE A LOVED one, pet, your home, job, career, a friendship or even your dignity, you must travel through all five stages of grief. Denial. Anger. Bargaining. Depression. And finally acceptance. How long you stay in each stage will differ for each person, each time. Sometimes you will jump back and forth between the first four stages. The most important aspect is that you *do* finish. Don't let yourself stay stuck in any of the stages longer than you need to.

⚜

$\mathcal{P}$EACE. IT DOES NOT REFER to a place where there is no pain, sorrow or difficulty. It means you can be amongst all that, and still be calm in your heart. Be kind. Be loving. Find the joy in everything and you will be led to peace!

☙

*F*ORGIVENESS MEANS YOU NO LONGER want to hold on to all the negative energy of anger bitterness and resentment. Forgiveness means you realize holding on is just hurting *you*. Forgiveness is the hardest life lesson to learn, and yet the *most* liberating and rewarding. Yes you were hurt - that is *life*. Now let it go so the lesson can be complete and *you* can *finally* move on!

⚓

ABSOLUTELY EVERYTHING IN THE WORLD has purpose. Bugs, trees, sand, ants and aunts. Anger, sadness, grief, and love. Do not worry if you do not understand the purpose of everything, just appreciate there IS a purpose, and it's not for you to judge or ridicule.

⚓

To LIVE IN HONESTY IS to appreciate nothing is more or less important than you.

☙

COMMON SENSE • *Louise Smith*

"ONLY AFTER THE LAST TREE HAS BEEN CUT DOWN. ONLY AFTER THE LAST RIVER HAS BEEN POISONED. ONLY AFTER THE LAST FISH HAS BEEN CAUGHT. ONLY THEN WILL YOU FIND THAT MONEY CANNOT BE EATEN."

~ *A Cree Prophecy.*

We are past the stage of thinking - it is time for action. Don't wait for another person, group or government for leadership. Create change yourself.

⚜

Sometimes the best thing you can do is absolutely nothing. If your gut/vibes/intuition isn't giving you clear directions, it could be because all the Divine t's haven't been crossed or i's dotted. Relax, wait and finding joy in this downtime might be the perfect thing to do.

⚓

"AT TIMES OUR OWN LIGHT GOES OUT AND IS REKINDLED BY A SPARK FROM ANOTHER PERSON. EACH OF US HAS CAUSE TO THINK WITH DEEP GRATITUDE OF THOSE WHO HAVE LIGHTED THE FLAME WITHIN US."

~ *Albert Schweitzer*

⚜

$\mathscr{I}$F IN YOUR GUT/INTUITION IT feels right and where you should be headed, then take the first step. Part of the mystery of life is moving toward what feels right, even though you may not know where you will end up. *Trust* your spirit knows even if your brain doesn't! As Martin Luther King said, 'you don't need to see the whole staircase before taking the first step.'

⚕

SURROUND YOURSELF WITH PEOPLE WHO are adventurous, loving, supporting and most of all kind. There are many fish in the sea and it makes no sense to hang on to the ones that fight against you or encourage you to fight and argue. (In a peaceful world, there is no need for fighting. About anything!) When you let the fighting relationships go, new wonderful, peaceful ones enter your life.

⚜

We automatically give a gift to *every* person we meet - but *we* choose what gift to give. Do you choose to give a smile, kind word, or a positive, loving or healing action? Or do you give anger, resentment, bitterness or superiority? We get what we give - so choose your gifts wisely.

⚜

ALWAYS TAKE TIME FOR YOURSELF. Do what *you* like to do. Think, watch, say and enjoy what tickles your fancy - without guilt, fear or anger! Too many, in their attempt to be the best friend, spouse, partner, fill their spare time with someone else's wants and desires. As nice as it is to support others, you'll never do it well, or with a fully open heart if you don't follow your heart as well.

⚓

LAUGH. EVERYDAY SEE THE HUMOUR in *everything!* Nothing is so bad, or so serious that something funny can't happen. Laughing forces you to breathe deeply, shake your body's energy system and push out the dark, negative air/energy/junk. The more you laugh the *healthier* and more content you'll be!

☙

*T*ODAY IS ABOUT TOLERANCE. IF everyone thought the same, did the same, spoke the same and looked the same, there would be no lessons, no learning and no tests to pass. How boring!

Today practice being less judgemental about someone else's differences by acknowledging they have just as much purpose on this earth as you, even if you have no idea why or what it could be.

☙

*T*ODAY IS A DAY TO remain centered and calm. No matter what transpires, even if it's rather stressful, your job is to remain calm and peaceful. Breathe slowly and deeply. Look for the positive. Take the path that allows you to stay clear of everyone else's hurricanes. Today practice controlling your inner energy and *be calm!*

☘

*Y*ESTERDAY IS DONE AND GONE. If you are still harbouring negative emotions from past moments, it means you have not yet learned the lessons from them. Stop and consider how living through it made you a better person, list the ways, and then *let it go.*

It's time to start living in *the now!*

Today is a whole new day - what do you want to do? Think? Accomplish? Work towards?

⚜

*F*EELING RESENTMENT WILL HOLD YOU back. It is poison that harms and hinders healing and forward movement on your journey. Today acknowledge one resentful feeling you need to release. Be open to discover the truthful reasons you are holding on to the anger - and then let go of these negative feelings and *free yourself.* Ending this cycle allows room for amazing new things to come into your life!

Letting go of the resentment doesn't mean you are 'forgetting' the pain. It means you have learned valuable lessons about yourself and humanity and you can move on, using those lessons to make a positive difference for yourself or others. (Remember, your anger holds you back, not the person or thing you are angry with.)

Knowing every soul has a purpose helps in the releasing stage. It's almost like looking at the situation through 3rd party eyes, saying 'I do not know why my soul (or my child's soul) desired to learn this lesson this way in this life, but I trust and accept there was a reason.'

$\mathcal{T}$ODAY IS THE DAY TO ponder your future.

Ask yourself this question, 'How am I resisting the 'new' that wants to manifest in my life?' Are you holding yourself back with 'that will never happen,' or 'it's just a dream,' thoughts? Are you allowing other people, places and things to hold you back?

Are you *really* open to living the life you dream of, or are they just empty words?

I have a friend who has always dreamed of moving out to the mountains. She has lived in the same small town her entire life, and has many reasons why she can't leave. Yet, when the opportunity comes up, and it often does, she holds firm to one of her reasons, even though she resents it. So, I wonder, is her dream 'empty words,' or is she allowing herself to be held back?

If it's empty words, she needs to let go of them and develop new, fitting dreams for her future. If she's allowing herself to be held back, she needs to build confidence that she *deserves* to live her dream, and then take one step at a time to bringing it to reality. If the path is the right one, she will be supported every step of the way.

So, today, ponder your future my friends.

Have fun!

☙

ONE OF THE MOST DIFFICULT things for a person to do is break free and go against the dominant thinking of their friends, and of the people they see every day. But to live in peace, joy and contentment, you *must* risk being different. Letting go of the need to 'fit in' frees you to discover who you really are, what your purpose is and the magical life that follows.

☙

$\mathscr{I}$T'S NOT ONLY 'OKAY' TO expect miracles, it's *highly encouraged!* Something will come into your life for the sole purpose of helping you heal and move forward on your journey. This person or thing may come for a long time or just a little. Ask for it - be open to it, and then express gratitude for the Divine occurrences of life, when the miracle is dropped on your path.

⚜

SOMETIMES YOU JUST HAVE TO let things go.

We all have moments where we feel mistreated, hurt or used. There will be times you will need to fight for your rights and there will be times you just need to acknowledge it's over, allow yourself to feel the pain and respectfully let it go and move on.

⚜

$\mathcal{B}$E OPEN TO CHANGING DIRECTIONS. Healing often depends on strength, willingness and ability to change directions. Far too many people put their own healing on hold due to fear or laziness, and then sit back and wonder why they are not happy or healthy. If you aren't waking up every morning saying *'my life is amazing,'* it's time once again to change the direction in an aspect of your life.

☩

Do you depend on others for happiness? Do you believe certain people or responsibilities are holding you back? Are you waiting for someone or something to lead you to the promised land?

Healing and living in a happy, content manner is a *solo endeavor*. Although others can/will support you, the path to contentment rests in *your hands*. Cut the negative cords of attachment and empower yourself!

⚜

$\mathcal{A}$s THE WINDS OF CHANGE grow in intensity and hurricanes brew all around you, remember to think before speaking. Words have a *powerful impact* and are never easily forgotten. Wounds inflicted by words of anger, blame, resentment and hate can last a long time.

If you want to be remembered for anything, let it not be foolish angry words.

⚜

*I*T IS ALWAYS BETTER TO say *no* when you need to - and *yes* when you want to. *Know the difference!!* If you always say yes, anger *will* creep in at some point and you *will* resent the person or the obligation. Stop yourself from feeling guilty when saying *no* - saying so is preserving the health of your body, mind and soul!

⚘

*T*HE WINDS OF CHANGE ARE always upon us. As they swirl around you, observe but do not absorb the hurricanes blowing near you. Do not let yourself be affected by the negative thoughts, actions and emotions of others. When others are angry, hurt or fearful, be mindful that you can continue to learn and love, but *do not attach* to the drama. Walk calmly in your truth!!

⚜

*L*OVE IS A STATE OF being, not an intellectual pro-cess reserved for specific times, people, places and things. Love is an energy that flows through your body *all the time* (whether you allow yourself to no-tice it or not)! When you *feel* gratitude, when you *feel* appreciation, even for the little things - like a sunny day, *that* is *love* energy connecting your mind, body and soul.

☙

TODAY SHED THE NEED TO complain. Whether you share them with others or keep it to yourself, the result is the same. Call it complaining, venting, whining or 'just being honest,' negative energy *will* bring you and others *down!*

Be honest in assessing whether are a complainer.

If yes - make it your pet project to look for the blessings in *everything!*

Remember - don't try to change others - just yourself.

*I*F MONEY WAS NO OBJECT, and failure was not a possibility...what would you do with your life?

✤

$\mathcal{A}$T SOME POINT IN TIME you have to stop blaming others for where you currently are in life (people, places, and things. Hometowns, parents, ex-spouse, boss, children, illness, etc.).

Blame is negativity.

It is dark energy that anchors you in the opposite place of peace, joy and contentment.

Left unattended, blame will fester and grow for so long you won't even remember what started it.

Instead of blaming, list all the lessons - things you learned about yourself, others and the world around you; things you would do differently if there was a next time; things you'll never do because they are hurtful.

Even list the ways you are stronger as a person.

Once this is complete, *let it go* and be grateful, yes, *grateful* for the lessons, for the wisdom gained, and that you finally 'got it' so you don't have to learn it again.

☙

*L*OOK AT HOW FAR YOU'VE grown in one year! Stay true to *your* dreams, goals and desires. If you have none - make some, for this world has an uncanny ability of giving us exactly what we ask for (if you expect misery, difficulty and problems, you'll get all three). Dream *big* - at worst you won't get it and will be no worse off than now - at best it will all magically land in your lap.

࿓

$\mathcal{E}$VERYDAY THE SUN RISES, STUFF happens, and the sun sets.

The rising and setting is out of your control, but some of the stuff isn't.

There are only so many 'days' that each of us are granted, and rarely do we know when we're in the last one.

So, why would you choose to work at a job you hate; fight for a failing relationship or hang around negative people that drain your energy?

The choice is yours.

⚜

$\mathcal{I}$ LEARNED IN THIS LIFE THAT I am much happier having less money and things, but more time, than when I had more money and things and less time.

☙

TREAT EVERYDAY LIKE ITS VALENTINE'S Day.

Everyday tell the people you love - that you love them.

Love even those that don't love you back.

Every day feel gratitude.

Everyday do and say kind things for those you know, and those you don't.

Everyday smile and be content with who and where you are.

Everyday dream amazing dreams of where you'll be tomorrow.

⚓

COMMON SENSE • *Louise Smith*

$\mathcal{K}$NOWING THAT REPEATING THE SAME actions will result in the same outcome, we must be willing to change things up if we expect a different result.

We have to stop and take a good long look at ourselves and the behaviours or attitudes that got us to where we are. When we start to see the patterns, we have to be willing to change things up if we want to end up somewhere different.

&cb;

A COMPLIMENT QUICKLY TURNS TO AN insult when you add the word 'but!'

⚓

$\mathscr{W}$HETHER WE ARE DRAGGED DOWN a difficult road, or whether we are living a life of peace and contentment, we all have the ability to make a difference. Given the current state of the world, making a difference is almost a social responsibility.

☙

WE ALL NEED A 'HAPPY place.' Whether that is an actual place or an activity, we need something where we can let the stresses of the moment wash away, allowing us to re-group, re-energize and feel peaceful once again.

⚜

$\mathcal{W}$E MUST LET GO OF the wounds from yesterday so that we can open our hearts and minds to the joys of today. Nothing positive comes from holding on to the wounds that have been inflicted upon us, they just stop us from seeing the wonderful moments in today.

⚓

We all live with lists in our head, including one with all the stupid/awful/anger-inducing/peeve-you-off/depressing things that happen every day. Every time something or someone grates on your nerve, whether you realize it or not, you add it to the list. As the day progresses this list gets bigger, longer and more intense. To the point, by days end you are in a foul mood from all the things listed on your imaginary 'Awful-list.'

We also have the capacity to keep a list in our head of all the great things that happen throughout the day. When we are feeling perfect and the world is spinning in a wonderful direction, it's easy to add items to this list.

What the majority of us don't do is keep both lists going simultaneously.

When the world seems to have it out for you it is more important than *ever* to keep a Great List.

By creating a Great List, your mind takes a break from the Awful List. Eventually you will find that you can't write down all the great things that happen every day. There are simply too many. As your Great List grows and over takes the Awful List in size, your attitude changes.

In essence, you train your mind to think and feel differently about the current state of your life. You will automatically be happier. More content. When you focus on what is good, even if they are only trivial

Common Sense • *Louise Smith*

little things, your mindset changes. You become positive, which attracts more positive.

And isn't that amazing. That *you* control the state of your own happiness regardless of what's happening out there in the world.

&

A PATH CAN SIMPLY BE THE direction you move. (e.g. when you come to a stop sign while driving, you have a choice, left, right or straight on through. You make your choice and this is then the 'path' you follow.)

The same applies to life. Every single thing that happens to us will move us in a direction. (e.g. someone says the sky is falling. To agree would take you down one path; to disagree, another; and to remain indifferent, another path again.)

The beauty is that we do have a say in most of the paths we follow. None are wrong - they only offer different experiences and lessons, with some leading to peace and contentment quicker than others.

WHEN LIFE IS OVERWHELMING AND challenges seem insurmountable – move to the back of the bus and let someone else do the driving for a while. By giving up control of life's driving, destination, speed and route, you open up to being led *exactly* where you are supposed to be. In the driver seat you see what's in front of you, at the back of the bus you see the world with a 360 degree perspective.

⚜

COMMON SENSE • *Louise Smith*

I WATCHED AND LISTENED TO A massive storm. Crashes of lightening, thunder booming and torrents of rain. It was *beautiful!*

Humans have tried to control the planet for centuries, but with what has been occurring around the globe as of late (earthquakes, volcanoes), the earth is not meant to be tamed or controlled by us.

We are wrong in assuming it needs to adapt to our needs – we need to adapt to it.

⚜

*L*ET TODAY BE THE DAY you stop feeling responsible to solve everyone else's problems. If you're not collecting a pay-cheque for it – it's not your job. Give yourself permission to put your needs first. You are worthy of it! You deserve it! Remember - you can't fit amazing new things in your life as long as it's filled with the junk of others.

⚓

COMMON SENSE • *Louise Smith*

*I*T'S A GREAT DAY TO clear the clutter. Pick a corner, closet or the car and clean it out. Don't stop there – move on to clearing out the clutter in friendships and relationships. If there are people who drain your energy, or don't treat you with the respect you deserve, *clear them out!* Your life fills with what you allow - so clear out the junk and allow only *great* things!

⚜

"THE THINGS YOU DO FOR YOURSELF IN LIFE DIE WITH YOU. THE THINGS YOU DO FOR OTHERS, LAST A LIFE TIME."

If it's a win/lose situation (they win, you lose), then it's not the right time for you to help. But if it's a win/win, then jump in with both feet. After all, making a difference on this planet is what gives your life purpose!

⚜

SOMETIMES WE GO THROUGH INCREDIBLY difficult times for the sole (and soul) purpose of allowing others to learn valuable lessons along their journey of life. Whether we realize this or not, this is one of the most amazing and self-less gifts we could ever give. Blessings to those who have and will walk this path!

⚓

APPRECIATE THE LITTLE THINGS - they are usually filled with incredible beauty.

I just ate breakfast on my deck and a gorgeous woodpecker came to join me. We both pecked away at our food for what seemed an eternity; peaceful, content, both of us enjoying the moment.

⚜

$\mathcal{B}$RONZE MEDALS GO TO THOSE who gracefully float through life, seemingly in the right spot at the right time. Gold medals go to those who make mistakes – massive ones; those who struggle, who learn lessons the hard way, and come out the other side letting go all bitterness, anger, resentment, and become *better*, kinder human beings!

⚜

KEEPING OUR BIG MOUTHS SHUT can sometimes be the longest and hardest lesson to learn. Here is a hint: you will never raise yourself higher by using words that cut another down. Being truthful is one thing, but if you think it's *ok* to hurt, wound or say anything that is mean-spirited, *you* haven't learnt the lesson yet.

⚜

I AM GRATEFUL. WHEN A MASSIVE thunderstorm stops me from mountain biking, I am still grateful because the earth needed the rain. In every disappointment, there are a multitude of blessings. You just need to notice them.

⚜

IF IT AIN'T BROKE, DON'T fix it.

D'uh!

But if it is broke and you want things to be different - then you must change (your attitude, actions, behaviour, words, thoughts, friends, expectations, strategy, etc).

If you don't, please don't be surprised to find yourself in exactly the same place you are right now... again and again and again.

⚓

A THOUSAND-PLUS TIMES A DAY THERE will be two paths to choose from.

1. Kindness - contentment.

2. Bitterness – jealousy – anger - resentment.

Choose wisely, for once you take the first few steps, it's harder and time consuming to turn around and re-trace where you came from in order to choose the other option. It's doable - just not as much fun!

⚜

*N*EVER DOUBT, IN ALL YOUR normalcy, in all your being just a regular guy/gal, that you *are* making an impact on the lives of others.

The only question you need ponder is this: Will I make a positive impact, or a negative one?

A question only you can answer.

⚓

*I*S IT CHALLENGING AND EVEN unpleasant to change a bad habit?

Yes.

Is it essential that you do so regardless?

Yes Yes Yes.

Today think of one negative habit you have (thinking negative thoughts, overeating, gossiping/trash-talking, being late, etc) and work on *changing* it. Success will be rewarded with a calmer, more peaceful life!

⚜

SMILE. THERE IS ALWAYS AT least one thing to smile about. A smile shares positive energy...allows stress to drift away...and brings sunshine even on rainy days. Besides, your smile may just make someone else's day.

⚓

*L*ook before you leap! Would moving forward, no matter how convincing others are, or how sweet the prospect, keep you *true to you?* If yes, maybe it's the right next step. If it's more about *their* needs than your own, take a breather, rest and look hard before deciding if you should leap. Stay true to yourself. If you don't know who you are - find out *before* leaping into someone else's dreams/plans.

⚜

I'T'S OKAY TO SAY NO! Say it as often as you need. Say it when you're stressed, super busy or simply when the request doesn't really interest you. Saying *no* to others usually means you are saying *yes* to yourself!

⚓

$\mathcal{I}$F YOU CAN'T BE TRUE to yourself who can you be true to? It's never easy looking in the mirror. You can like *or* hate what you see - either way it's all you get in this life journey. Accept and find peace, love and contentment - or hate and find anger, bitterness and resentment. What you *feel about yourself* will follow you wherever you go, especially in *all* of your relationships! It's your life - and ultimately your choice.

⚜

ON'T BE AFRAID TO BE prudently selfish today (focused on self, not others). It might be exactly what you need to do if you are to understand and heal yourself. Sometimes we ignore our own needs by staying busy with everyone else's. Although great for others, it *blocks* you from learning your lessons, healing and being content!

⚜

*T*ODAY IS AS GOOD A day as any to accept the challenges of life. Reflect on past experiences, remembering that obstacles are what help us grow. It is human nature to choose between being bitter or better. Today reflect on all your bitter experiences and *make peace* with them. Let go of anger, bitterness and resentment. Now is the time to be better.

⚜

"PEACE - IT DOES NOT MEAN TO BE IN A PLACE WHERE THERE IS NO NOISE, TROUBLE OR HARD WORK. IT MEANS TO BE IN THE MIDST OF ALL THOSE THINGS AND STILL BE CALM IN YOUR HEART."

(unknown author)

Positive love/energy is easier received by your loved ones when you, the sender are in a place of peaceful calm, not absorbing the drama, but observing.

⚓

ODAY IDENTIFY ONE SMALL CHANGE you've been postponing that could improve your life. It could be big - like ending a relationship, or small, like switching laundry detergents. Change can be frightening, and sometimes we postpone even the small changes because intuitively we know they can ignite powerful ones.

⚜

IT IS IMPORTANT TO REMEMBER you are greater than your physical body. Greater than your human accomplishments and defeats.

You existed before you came here, and will exist long after you leave.

Part of the journey is to find balance between what your spirit already knows and what your human self thinks it knows.

⚜

*Y*OU CANNOT CONTROL WHAT ANOTHER person says, does or thinks. You can only control *your* reactions to it. You control your own thoughts/feelings/attitudes to what happens to you, but you cannot control the actual events. It is important to learn the difference.

☨

COMMON SENSE • *Louise Smith*

*H*ONOUR ALL RELATIONSHIPS WITH LOVING care and attention. A relationship is a living thing fully in the present. It grows, changes, flows through many cycles and sometimes even ends. Whether intimate or friendship-based, be aware to continually renew your relationships through kind, loving actions.

Never assume that a single kind action of the past is enough to sustain a relationship indefinitely. And for those relationships that do end, honour the ending, feel gratitude for the lessons learned, and walk with confidence to the next cycle that is waiting for you.

Life is a process of learning. Sometimes there are a multitude of lessons all at the same time. It's always best to ponder our own actions, thoughts and words. It is in that process where we will see the les-

COMMON SENSE • *Louise Smith*

sons presented, and whether we learned them. Others that share experiences with us are merely divine tools to help us learn. Once we've 'passed,' we can feel nothing but gratitude for having the experience that got us to our new level of enlightenment. What an amazing journey it is!

AWARENESS.

Appreciation.

Gratitude.

I learned long ago these three things make up happiness.

Be aware of wonderful things happening all around you every day (and there will be many).

Appreciate that you noticed them. Not everyone does.

Feel gratitude. For everything, good and bad. It's how lessons are learned and souls progress!

⚜

To ACCOMPLISH GREAT THINGS, WE must dream, plan, act, but most importantly *believe*. The believing is the hardest part, harder than any of the lesson-related roadblocks put in your way. To reach utopia, you must believe with all your heart and soul that you are worth it, and that it's possible. Breathe it, feel it, relish in it, and *then* it will become reality.

⚜

NEVER DOUBT YOUR LIFE HAS purpose greater than working, eating, sleeping and being.

Although we read with awe at those who create a better world in gargantuan ways, there is just as much importance to those whose purpose is to greet everyone with kindness, keep nature beautiful, or fill our ears with music.

Every soul has purpose; some just need to be uncovered.

⚜

$\mathcal{T}$ODAY I AM THANKFUL FOR broken hearts. In that moment of pain, we learn we *are* capable of great *love*. And if we felt love once, we can and will feel love again. There is no room in True Love for jealousy, anger, resentment, bitterness, or a need/desire to control. True Free Love is filled with joy, contentment, peace and calm. *Always*.

My advice would be to love as much as possible. Love is not just for intimate partners, it's an emotion and a feeling to be shared with many. Love siblings, friends, nature, activities. Love as much as you possibly can - it will fill your life with amazing joy and contentment. When you fill your head and heart with loving thoughts, negativity has a hard time finding a place to anchor inside you. When you reach the point of loving everything freely, others will feel free to love you too.

⚓

WHEN YOU FEEL FRAZZLED, YOUR mind spinning, your emotions up and down and almost anything can set you off – it's time to get grounded. Put your feet on the ground; get some fresh air; sweat; dig in the dirt; play with rocks; listen to birds sing. Touching base with the natural world will settle your racing energy and balance your mind, body and spirit.

⚜

YOUR WAY ISN'T THE ONLY way. Life is a journey and there are many roads to get to the same place. If your way works for you - wonderful! But do not judge another because he takes a different path. You never know - he may get there even faster! Be confident in the path you choose - if you aren't - simply change directions and find something that fits you better.

☙

WHETHER YOU ARE AWARE OF it or not, you will encounter numerous spiritual teachers in your life. They will provide you with all the techniques, motivation, and inspiration to live a life of total peace, calm and contentment - *but* that is not enough. Ultimately it is a personal journey and only *you* can take steps to get there. I hope you do - it's simply *bliss!*

WISDOM IS ACHIEVED SLOWLY. You will go through a never-ending assortment of experiences in life, each offering you the opportunity to learn lessons that make you and others better, kinder humans. When you complete these lesson cycles and feel gratitude (even and especially when they were difficult), *that* is how wisdom grows.

☩

*T*ODAY EXAMINE WHETHER YOUR CONNECTIONS with others leave you empowered or disempowered. Are you always giving to others in hopes you'll be appreciated? Sadly it doesn't work that way. You cannot 'give' with hopes of 'getting' something in return, not even love. Empower yourself by giving *freely* with absolutely *no* expectations, not even a thank you - then you will have mastered the art of kindness.

⚜

*P*AY CLOSE ATTENTION TO YOUR gut feelings. It's less important to know *why* you feel a *no* or a *yes*, and more important to just *follow it!* Our gut feelings/vibes/intuition are our natural GPS steering systems for the journey of life. They will always bring you exactly where you are supposed to be. Directions can change daily - so check in often!

⚓

$\mathcal{B}$E CAREFUL WHAT YOU WISH for. Sometimes the things you utter under your breath end up landing in your lap.

⚓

COMMON SENSE • *Louise Smith*

$\mathcal{E}$VERYONE IS 'LOVABLE.'

The best way for others to easily love you is to love yourself first.

Love life.
Love the simple things.
Love the air you breathe.

Love saying and doing kind things for others, not because it 'elevates' you, but because it just feels right.

Love everything.

When you do this, love will easily find its way to you!

*W*HEN THERE IS SORROW, THERE is also joy. The two cannot exist without each other, each taking a rightful place on your journey. Be careful not to be so caught up in your sorrow that you miss those magical, joyous and sometimes hilarious moments. Look for them, relish in them and give thanks for the balance along the way.

"I FEEL INSPIRATION IS OF PARAMOUNT IMPOR-TANCE. IF I CAN INSPIRE SOMEONE, AND IF THAT PERSON ALSO CAN INSPIRE ME, THEN WE CAN DO MANY GOOD THINGS FOR THE BETTERMENT OF THIS WORLD."

~ *Sri Chinmoy*

I couldn't possibly have said this better myself. Enjoy the magic of today.

⚓

$\mathcal{S}$PEND TIME WITH THE ONES you love.

Show them or tell them you love them as much as possible!

You never know when 'life' will out rank you and your other priorities, and the chance will be gone.

☙

"Jealousy is a disease, love is a healthy condition. The immature mind mistakes one for the other, or assumes the greater the love, the greater the jealousy. In fact, they're almost incompatible; one emotion hardly leaves room for the other. Both at once can produce unbearable turmoil."

~ R. Heinlein

Release fear and be confident in self - this will lead you away from jealousy and toward love.

⚓

$\mathcal{W}$HEN MY BROTHER DIED,

I thought it would seem like he was way over there,

and I was way over here.

There would be mountains, valleys and oceans between us.

And after a bit I realized he was NOT over there, separate from me.

He was here.

In me.

Around me.

COMMON SENSE • *Louise Smith*

All the time.

And thus began a new relationship with him.

I found out,

he never left,

he just changed the way he stayed.

⚓

MAKING UNKIND COMMENTS ABOUT ANOTHER, whether they can hear you or not - even if it is said under the guise of humour, is just plain mean!

It's another example of negative, dark energy.

Never judge another person for what he says, does, or thinks.

He has his own lessons to learn and purpose in this life, even if you don't/can't understand what that purpose could be.

⚜

WHEN HEARTFELT AND SINCERE, TWO simple words can change everything. Make it your goal to say them at least 100 times today. Smile when doing so, the energy inside and out will automatically change to positive!

Thank you!

⚕

THERE IS MORE TO YOUR life than eating, working, errands and laundry.

If yours was a perfect world, what would you be doing, where would you be doing it, and how happy would you be?

Now is the time to get out of the comfort of your routine and take one step toward your dream. Tomorrow, take another. Then another.

You'll never get anywhere if you don't take that first step.

⚜

IN THE BEGINNING THERE IS a seed,
a thought,
a dream,
an idea.

The journey unfolds as each step is taken.
There will be struggles,
changes,
the unexpected.

But THIS is the journey of life!

Enjoy,
revel in it,
plant many seeds,
and be thankful.

For when you reach the end,
this part is over.

You will have learned the lessons,
passed the tests,
and will graduate to the Other Side.

⚜

YOU ARE NOT HERE BY accident or by a coincidence of nature. Whether you know it or not, your life has deep meaning and a profound purpose. Start with living life in a state of contentment *every day* - and the purpose will unfold before you. Trust you can and *will* leave your mark in the most wonderful of ways!

⚜

It's Time to Say Goodbye

I had lunch with a wonderful friend before she headed out to the east coast of Canada for an undetermined period of time. Understandably, she was excited about the adventure that lay ahead of her and I too got caught up in the wonder of it all as we said goodbye.

Life is like that. We often find ourselves having to bid farewell, sometimes with relief, and other times with great sadness.

One of my more difficult goodbyes came when my brother passed away a few years ago. I was filled with the typical emotions of a mourning sister, wondering why on earth something like this would happen, and how much I didn't want him to be gone.

In truth, our lives are a series of cycles. There will be many beginnings and many ends. We will have cycles with our jobs, loved ones, relationships, homes and even friends. Some cycles will last a long time, and others just for a moment. Each serves a purpose in making us who we are.

When I first re-entered the corporate world after my kids marched off to elementary school, I found the perfect company to work for. Every aspect of my job was fulfilling and a pleasure.

Then one day it just didn't seem to fit anymore. No matter how hard I tried, my office mojo was gone.

I found less and less pleasure with the projects I worked on. Nothing inspired me. The harder I tried to make things click, the more road blocks were set up in front of me.

One day I woke up. I realized the cycle of that job was finished, the lessons learned, and it was time for me to move on. Once I acknowledged that, everything for the next work-related cycle started falling into place.

The same can be said for those who are ending relationships. Sometimes you hold on for dear life even though you sense or know something isn't quite right.

Regardless of the reason we stay holding on to the last threads, we all have signs thrown in our path the end is near, and it's time to make a change.

This is the thought I want to leave all of you with.

The completion of a cycle is natural and must be allowed to occur. Holding on to something or some-

COMMON SENSE • *Louise Smith*

one past the proverbial due date only holds you back from something even better. Something that includes the next lessons of your life.

Even when you have no idea what the future holds. No idea who you will share time with, what you will do, or where you will end up, you need to let go, say goodbye and move forward, trusting that everything will one day make sense.

Much like my change of jobs. Once that cycle was complete I headed in an entirely different direction. It was filled with bliss, accomplishment and a true feeling of purpose.

So how do you know when a cycle is coming to an end?

If you are open and honest with yourself, you will feel it. You will see the signs that something is amuck. Your blissful feeling that 'all is well with the world' will be replaced with the beginnings of restlessness.

As though there is something missing but you can't put your finger on it.

You may even start to feel irritated. The person, job or home you once loved and adored will suddenly seem to speak another language and as time goes on you'll find it more and more difficult to connect.

The longer you ignore the signs, the less and less you'll have in common, until you get to the point you wonder why you made that choice in the first place.

So, let it go. Even if you have absolutely no idea what will happen next, acknowledge that cycle, friendship, relationship, job, or home is over, and there is something new and even better waiting for you.

When I finally finished the cycle of grief after my brother died, a new and wonderful cycle began. I was so afraid that saying goodbye would mean I no longer had a connection with him, and once I truly let go and bid farewell, I discovered he never left. He just changed the way he stayed.

I am certain of a couple things. One, whether each of these new cycles lasts a day, a month, a year, or a lifetime, I know they are meant to be.

Two, I am certain the people, relationships, friends and interests from old cycles will stay in our lives if they are meant to. And those who have completed their cycle with us will drift away, following their own path.

Birth and death. The cycle of life. Goodbyes and hellos.

Everything begins and everything ends. We need to move forward in our lives with confidence the lessons we learn serve a purpose in making us who we are meant to be.

Much, much love and deepest respect,
Louise

About the Author

Louise Smith is an avid mountain biker, hiker and outdoor enthusiast. After a successful career in marketing, keynote speaking and corporate training, she has semi-retired to a chalet 'in the north.'

Louise lives every day as though it could be her last. Nothing is ever so bad she can't see the good in it. She endeavours to make each person she comes into contact with feel as though they are special. Usually they are.

After the SMA (spinal muscular atrophy) diagnosis of her niece Rebecca, Louise gathered friends and family to organize a fundraising event to support cure and treatment research. 2010 marked the ninth anniversary of the Esso Rebecca Run for SMA, which in conjunction with the Angel Gala for SMA (also inspired by Rebecca), has now raised over $1.7 million dollars.

In 2009 Louise published her first book, Death and the Lessons I Learned after nearly drowning in a fresh water lake.

These days Louise enjoys working outdoors in a resort environment, and playing in the trails with fellow mountain bike enthusiasts.

You can find out more about Louise at:

www.rebeccarun.com
www.angelgala.com
www.thelessonsoflife.com

A portion of every book sale is donated to SMA treatment and cure research.

A generous donation has been made to both the
Gwendolyn Strong Foundation and the Families of
Spinal Muscular Atrophy for each copy of this work
sold by our friends at Stovetopcover.com

www.ingramcontent.com/pod-product-compliance
Lightning Source LLC
Chambersburg PA
CBHW022016090426
42739CB00006BA/166